The Empowered Solo Parent

Infused with seahorse positive energy,
so that any negative subjects covered
transmute into good vibes

written
by Cheryl Cooke

Birthed in June 2016
whilst pregnant with my son Xander

1

The Empowered Solo Parent
ISBN 9781787231351
Copyright © 2017 Cheryl Cooke

First Edition 2017

There are two ways copyright applies to this book. Feel free to ascribe to the one that you prefer. They both work, but in different worlds.

The New Way
If you by chance come across a copy of this book without paying for it, buy a print or an ebook copy and gift it to someone else. All reviews also help to keep things spinning. Good ones make an author's day. Not so good ones help authors improve their writing. This all helps to keep everything in karmic balance.

The Traditional View

Disclaimer
The purpose of this book is to educate and entertain. The author and publisher of this book do not dispense medical or psychological advice. You should not use the techniques herein for treatment of any physical or medical issues without seeking the advice of a qualified medical practitioner.

In the event you use any advice from this book, the author and publisher assume no responsibility for your actions.

Front cover images ©pani_yana and ©caan2gobelow from Adobe Stock.

Extract about the seahorse from The Germinatrix and Other Tall Tales used with kind permission of Tom Evans.

Dedicated to my angelic daughter Zara, my magical son Xander and to all who give birth

Contents

Chapter 1 : Birth of this Book

Empowering our inner strength - Forgiving ourselves

*"The weak can never forgive. Forgiveness is the
attribute of the strong."*
~ Mahatma Gandhi

My husband and I married in November, when I was 3
months pregnant with my daughter and first born Zara.

We were planning to get married in Cuba on the beach
but when I found out I was pregnant, our plans changed
and we brought our wedding forward to November, and
decided the registry office would be adequate. We were
married on a small budget. However, all our family and
friends were in attendance so it was positive from that
viewpoint.

I think not getting the wedding we wanted, down to
not having the dress and rings we desired either was the
start of our difficult marriage.

Not that any of this really matters, because it is not
the wedding day that counts. It is the marriage and how

much both people are willing to put into that partnership.

I don't want to write too much about the past, and the negative experiences because my aim for this book is to help others with the challenges that come up as a solo parent. Also, these days I prefer to focus my mind mainly on the positive as I have learnt that when we go too deeply into the negative it will attract more of this into our life experience.

I didn't even take on my husband's surname, which may have been another sign of things to come!

However, whatever it was, our journey was about to begin. Zara was born on 2nd June 2011 at midday. I had a very positive home birth experience in a birthing pool using hypnobirthing techniques. I will go into more detail in chapter 11 about my birth story and our famous five minutes!

Soon after the birth, my husband and I began having problems. He didn't take well to becoming a father and to be honest I struggled becoming a mother too! So, we were both having our own issues.

I believe there are always two sides to these stories, nobody should take 100% of the blame.

I have learned through the process and now I am at the point I am at on my journey, that we must take a long hard look at ourselves and realise that everything that happens in our lives, is attracted into our life experience by our thoughts, feelings and behaviours.

This is very harsh truth for many to face, but it is the truth and for any real progression in life we must realise this if we want the results we desire in life.

I am currently divorcing my husband for unreasonable behaviour due to his emotional and financial abuse that endured for 5 years. I have let go and forgiven all of this now, so talking about it is much easier. However, I prefer to touch more on positives and send him love in my thoughts and actions now. As this works so much better than directing anger and resentment towards him. I will also speak more about this in future chapters.

Two things our marriage lacked; communication and trust. Without these the marriage, cannot be sacred. The support and love was disappearing.

He would display neglectful and abusive behaviour. Turning up home late regularly after drinking and spending our money. He would steal my credit cards and money from my wallet and our joint account would have no funds to cover our bills.

There was no security or safe place for me as a new mother, and this was tough.
I felt like a single mother even when married and living together.

It took me many years of procrastinating to eventually decide to close myself down emotionally and to make plans to end our marriage. At a later date, further in this book, whilst writing my statement of case for our divorce I realised that I had held on to guilt for not leaving him at the time that he turned up with our daughter at 7 months old accompanied by police due to his drink driving accident with her in the car! I did lots of work on forgiving myself for staying so long after this event!

My daughter was 4 years old when I eventually achieved our separation in October 2015. He did not leave easily and it took police and my social worker involvement to achieve this.

The start of my solo parent journey had begun! Many challenges were ahead. Visits to information offices to get advice about divorce and child maintenance and any financial help that was available to single parents. It was a minefield to me. All this whilst trying to work part time on my health and massage business and do all the house and parenting tasks alone, this was all very challenging and exhausting work!

The first time I let my husband take our daughter overnight after our separation was difficult. He had just got his driving license back and I really did not trust him to take her in the car with him. I cried for so long after he drove off, and even called ahead to his mother (who he was staying with) to ensure she arrived safely with him! I was so scared for my little girl. Luckily his mother called me later to say they had arrived perfectly fine.

My daughter and I had just got used to living in the family home without my husband and then in December we were asked by our letting agent, if we could move out in February. Landlords wanted the house back!

Christmas 2015 was a strange time, as it was our first Christmas without my husband, and my single parent journey was young. I spent Christmas day at my parents' home in Somerset with my daughter. It was an emotional time.

I realise that going into too much detail about the bad things that happened isn't going to help anyone reading this book or writing it.

Please just understand that the five years we were married was in no way smooth. It had plenty of downs. A few ups of course, but mainly I felt lonely, unsupported and abused in many ways.

I realise now that happiness is an inside job. That we do attract all our experiences to us. Good or bad. Negativity brings bad experiences and positivity brings the good ones.
We all have pasts, and these bring about our future. However, we must remain present.

Be conscious about our thoughts and feelings and how we are projecting into the world.

Everything and everyone around us is a mirror of our past thoughts and when we realise this we can really begin to notice how we have been in the past.

What is most important is to ask yourself questions. Why is this happening? What am I feeling? To work through our emotions and feel them, and clear out this old energy so that we can move forward more evolved and stronger and more real. Being true to ourselves and who we are is essential to living a more fulfilled and happy existence.

Love is the most important thing, and learning that loving unconditionally is the only way can take time. Being conscious is essential and realising that our actions and states of mind matter, because we are so deeply interconnected with one another.

Whenever there is negativity around we need to learn that the only way it can affect us is if we vibrate at that lower frequency. If we choose to vibrate higher in a more positive energy, then it cannot influence us.

Every experience that comes along is an opportunity to learn and grow. To let go of old beliefs and welcome the new.

If we learn from our experiences, then they were never wasted.

It is important to forgive ourselves and others for whatever has happened. This is the best way to clear it and grow stronger to attract better into our lives.

I felt guilty for a long time about staying so long and not leaving when I first realised our marriage was never going to work.

However, I had to forgive myself and my husband for we both only did what we felt best at that point in time.

I am truly grateful for the part my husband played in my life journey, he pushed the buttons that were required to bring out my issues that were to be healed to further my growth.

Lesson: Forgiveness

It is important to forgive ourselves and others for whatever has happened. This is the best way to clear it and grow stronger to attract better into our lives.

Daily Affirmation

I lovingly forgive myself and others. I am Free.

Chapter 2 : A New Love

Learning curves – Vulnerability is good

*"Being vulnerable is the only way to allow your heart
to feel true pleasure."*
~ *Bob Marley*

In January, I was busy planning a house move to our new home in February. After viewing several houses, I finally find a two-bed house in Ash through a massage client that I was treating.

So, in the process of packing and sorting out changes of addresses and post forwarding. I also needed to get some quotations for cleaning the carpets for the end of tenancy clean that is part of any tenant's duties in a tenancy agreement.

So, I decided to put out my requirements for a carpet cleaner on Facebook.

An acquaintance sent me a contact and I followed it up with a phone call. The carpet cleaner came over that week to carry out the estimate. When I answered the door, I was crying and in quite a vulnerable state! After coming off the phone from my ex-husband who at the time was still giving me many challenges! I also had a big red sore sty on my left eye, so did not look at my best!

Whilst walking around my home we talked and seemed to have a deep connection, the energy between us was magnetic.

Later that evening the carpet cleaner messaged me with a sweet request, asking if he was crossing the line, but would I like to go out for dinner with him. Well of course I felt quite flattered and due to the amazing energy between us I accepted the dinner invite.

I realised that even though I had been at my worst state, no make up and a sty on my eye, crying floods of tears! I had been vulnerable and real. This was strangely attractive to a man. They like to be our protectors and always like to help.

This realisation I had months later, did make sense. A man likes a vulnerable woman that they can be helpful to. That doesn't mean they like a needy woman, far from it. They just like to see our feminine side so they can demonstrate their masculine side.

This new man in my life, really did like to help out. He was amazing and a real god send after the turmoil I had been through. We spent most weekends together and began to get close.

Shared our dreams and our fears. Spoke about our pasts. He even gave me some parenting tips about ensuring my daughter didn't take over.

Playing both roles as a solo parent can be tough at times, so having this new man that came with great advice to help with this really was a gift from the angels!

Next comes my house move, and then a real shocker that really turns my life upside down. However, everything happens for a reason and I truly believe this now!

Lesson: Vulnerability

This realisation I had months later, did make sense. A man likes a vulnerable woman that they can be helpful to. That doesn't mean they like a needy woman, far from it. They just like to see our feminine side so that they can demonstrate their masculine side.

Daily Affirmation

It is safe to feel. I open myself to life. I am willing to experience life.

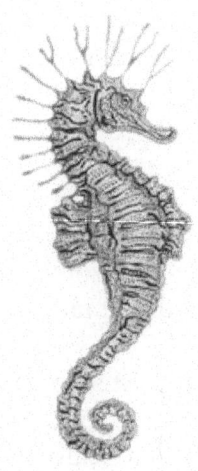

Chapter 3 : Moving House

De-cluttering – Making space for the new

"Let go. Why do you cling to pain? There is nothing you can do about the wrongs of yesterday. It is not yours to judge. Why hold on to the very thing which keeps you from hope and love?"
~ *Leo Buscaglia*

On 14th February 2016, we moved to our new house in Ash. Leaving a nice big 3 bed semi for a small 2 bed terrace home was the first part of my letting go process!

Downsizing was not easy! I literally lost three big rooms, which including a conservatory, an extra bathroom and a bedroom which I used as my massage room for treating my clients! I felt like a snake shedding its skin.

Yes, I was getting a fresh start. However, letting go of so much luxurious space was very tough! Especially the massage room! In my new home, I had to treat clients in my lounge which meant taking the couch down all the time after each client. Cannot compare to having a treatment room already set up the way you want it!

It was the inconvenience of it all that made it such a tough transition!

I really did like my 3-bed family home in Farnham so it was quite difficult accepting this move.

Especially as the new home wasn't exactly what I wanted. Not to mention that all my things did not fit into the new small house! When the removal men left all my belongings on the lounge floor and they stacked up to the ceiling it was quite a shocker! I had to find places for all these material possessions! What a headache!

To top it all off, the garden was flooded and there was not any heating or hot water working in the new property. It took the new landlords four days to fix these issues too. So, this created a lot of stress and tension for my new start.

I don't think that any of this helped my new relationship to flourish. My poor man didn't know how to handle me when I was stressed. He carried many insecurities from his past and it had not helped him to be strong for others.

The cracks in our relationship started to show. However, what was really happening was that we had both had insecure childhoods. So now we were triggering each other. So, when the going got tough emotionally my new knight in shining armour was now doing a runner!

During the two weeks that he had ran from us, I discovered that I had fallen pregnant. Shocker! Details to follow in the next chapter!

My lessons from moving house were that letting go is a major process.

Lesson: De-cluttering and letting go to make space for new

De-cluttering is in fact very cleansing, and it does make room for new and better things to come into your life. It also helps to close the chapter on your old life and is therapy for letting go.

Daily Affirmation

It is with love that I totally release the past. I am free. I am love.

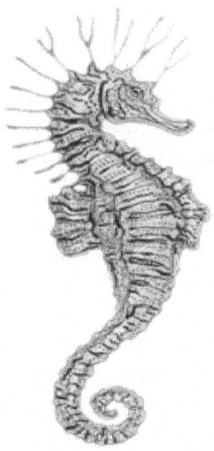

Chapter 4 : Coping Strategies

Pregnancy while single – Keep the faith

"It is through gratitude for the present moment that the spiritual dimension of life opens up."
~ *Eckhart Tolle*

In May 2016, my new love decided to do another runner out of my life. Just one week before my 12-week baby scan.

For weeks, he had tried to entice me to abort the baby. He said he didn't want a child of his own. However, while we had been in loving embraces he had told me very different, saying on occasions that he wanted a baby with me, and if he had not impregnated me this time he would have tried again because he was so in love with me. He also said many times that he loved being part of a ready-made family with me and my daughter.

This man did not know himself what he really wanted in life. To be honest, I now realise that he was a mirror for myself, as I had also been confused about what I wanted too.

This was a very traumatic time for me. Facing the fear of being alone whilst pregnant was very unsettling and I really did go through some dark times.

My worst time was when I crashed heavily one Sunday when my daughter was playing up, she was being very demanding because she could sense my energy of loss I think.

I felt very depressed and out of control. I was having a mini breakdown. The day gradually got worse and worse and I sank deeper and deeper until a friend felt so concerned they called the police. So, I had a visit from them. They wanted me to go to hospital for a mental assessment. However, I refused to go, as this was the last thing I wanted.

The policeman said he could not leave me alone in the state I was reported to have been in, so he asked me to call a friend to come over and sit with me. This satisfied their protocols and the policeman finally left.

My friend stayed for a while and comforted me. I also made an appointment at the doctors for the next day. Although that wasn't much help. All the doctor wanted to do was prescribe me some anti-depressant medication!

This was indeed my turning point. It woke me up. I decided to go against the medical system and called on my light-worker/energy worker friends to do some therapy on me. This was exactly what my soul needed to move on and let go of the situation I found myself in.

I learnt there is nothing you can do to change or control others. All you can do is change yourself and control how you deal with situations in your life.

I am blessed that I know so many amazing therapists, coaches and mediums, but also that so many of them are my friends. One of my closest friends that I met over 15 years ago, started as my life coach back then, she has been there with wise words all through my challenging journey.

I have also grown an amazing support network which I am sure I will receive so much help from when baby arrives in November.

Many things have kept me going through this process, my daughter has been a real blessing to me, she is such a sensitive soul and has been very strong and supportive considering she is only 5 years old.

I was also lucky enough to be given free life coaching sessions from a client of mine, which even as I write this book I am still enjoying learning and strengthening through. I will detail more about the life coaching in a chapter to follow.

I also reluctantly joined a single parents group in Guildford. I say reluctantly because I didn't want to put a label on myself and remain in this place. I want a family unit, with a supportive man one day. Remaining single for too long is not part of my life plan. However, I am learning to go with the flow much more and I know that the universe will send what is right for me when timing is of divine nature. I am now working on me, and focusing on what I want.

I have spent much time doing energy work and hypnosis to remove blocks from childhood and past lives. This has been a tiring journey and has helped me very much. We really do need to go within to find our happiness. Only our souls know what is meant for us.

I made a good friend at the parenting group and in a future book I will interview other solo parents about their journeys

Part of my life coaching was to find a support network and to plan days out with my daughter and get used to doing things on my own.

I learnt to play with my daughter more which helped us to connect at a deeper level, and our relationship is so much stronger.

It is very empowering when you learn to do so much on your own. You realise that your needs for a man to help with it all are so much less once you give yourself the confidence to do it all yourself.

Yes, life would be easier in many ways with a supportive partner around to lighten the load, however at times, especially if they are not the right fit for you and your family, it can make things harder when they are around. Especially when you have a child like mine that really picks up on energy of others. She could always tell when things were off balance. Then she would play up and things would be very stressful.

I learned so much about myself through this process and more about my life path and what my divine purpose is in this life.

Firstly, I learned how to be an earth mother, that treats her children naturally and is very conscious about her parenting and health.

Secondly, I discovered how to be a guide and teacher to others for health in pregnancy and for children's health.

I have decided that I will divert my career more towards teaching parents about using natural medicine for the health of their family. This will empower them in times of stress when children are unwell.

I have visited many psychic fairs and holistic events, where I have met some more friends and contacts for therapy and guidance.

My last reading by a medium was very encouraging and inspired me to believe that all will work out the way I want it to. I just need to keep my dreams in focus and keep the faith.

On the days when I felt low or not too well through my pregnancy, I tried to seek guidance from within myself, use my intuition more. However, if this did not help I knew I always had a good friend / therapist/healer I could call on for the right help at that time.

Focusing on gratitude for the things you already have in your life really does help each day, and writing down the things I have done well, as giving yourself praise is always a great way to make you feel good.

At my second scan, at 20 weeks, the father turned up to see the baby on the scan. Like he did at 12 weeks too.

He seems to want to be involved with the baby and to do his best. Which considering he never wanted it before was a real improvement.

I used various techniques to help my anxiety about facing him at each scan, some given to me by the life coach and others were advice from my long-term friend who said to always remain in your heart space, sending good vibes and love towards the father and the situation. Always helps to visualise a positive outcome too.

At the 20-week scan we found out that I was in fact having a boy. Which was great news. I had intuition that it would be a boy anyway so I was very pleased. Also, to see how healthy it was, measuring correctly and moving well, was a real comfort.

The father seemed very happy and he acted positively towards me. We both went home with smiles on our faces. Later that evening we text messaged each other, with kind words. Apologies to each other for the pain we had put each other through and words that we are going to do our best for this little child. He even admitted that we were good together before.

A few days later I asked if he would be willing to help out with a few jobs for me to help ease the load, he was only too pleased to accommodate.

So now we have this relationship where we are both here for the baby (maybe me a little more so!) and seem to be on good terms.

I have however realised that we may not be best suited to one another, and I am happy to just let things be and have faith in what may be.

I have faced many challenges whilst on this pregnancy journey, and I have been strong enough to deal with them all and very effectively most of the time.

It is so important to focus on the things we do well as a parent. Especially when we are doing both roles as father and mother.

My daughter and I have a very strong and healthy relationship and I am very proud of this. She is growing into a well-rounded beautiful individual inside and out. I am so proud of her too. She is very excited about her baby brother coming into the world. She will be an amazing sister.

I decided within one of my coaching sessions, that I would hold a summer party to thank all my close friends for all their help throughout my last year of challenges and to ask for their continued support when baby arrives. This was also a house warming to bring good energy into my new home, so many reasons for a good party! I love parties and I love friends. They are my family. I love them all so very much.

My message to all single parents is to ensure you have a large support network of good friends that you know you can call on in times you need that little extra help.

Lesson: Gratitude

I am grateful for my lovely spiritual kind loving friends. They are all so different and so amazing. I am very blessed to know all of them.

Daily Affirmation
Every day I give thanks for all that I have in my life.

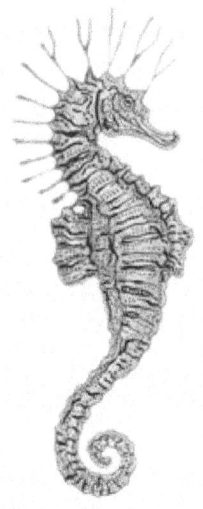

Chapter 5. Letting Go

Moving on – Forgiveness

"You must learn to let go. Release the stress. You were never in control anyway."
~ Steve Maraboli

I realised very early on in my separation with my husband that letting go and not feeling bitter is one of the greatest gifts you can give to yourself and others. Really forgiving someone that has appeared to have wronged you is a difficult process, however the alternative of holding on to resentment and anger is much worse.

It is also very important to forgive yourself, because of course it is always 50/50 in relationships and so you cannot place complete blame on the other or yourself. It is best to look inside of yourself and question why did this happen to me? What could I have done better?

Looking in the mirror at yourself and truly seeing what and who you are is the best healing process there is, it is very enlightening and does help so much with spiritual growth.

They say that when you have experienced real pain and trauma you discover the most about yourself and I know this to be completely true now.

It is so satisfying to discover your true self and find out what it is you really want from life.

Every time I feel myself going into negative lower vibration energy, I try to shift it by feeling it and asking myself questions about why I am feeling this, what is this about and it is a great way to shift those past pains and heal so that you can truly move on.

It is not an overnight process; it can take months to years to heal and truly discover yourself again.

Focusing on what we want as opposed to what we do not want is a great way to attract a better life. Sending positive vibes, good thoughts and love to others and to yourself, staying in your heart space is so powerful in achieving what you want. You can affect how others act by controlling how you act and feel. What we put out is what we get back – always!

Constant visualisations, intentions and meditations around the things you want are very powerful and at times you can see the results of this way of life coming back to you very quickly and you realise that this actually does work.

The more time we spend moaning about what happened to us the more we are likely to attract the same experiences again and again.

I find it amazing how the universe sends us evidence of our work into our reality. Have you ever thought about someone and then a few days later you bump into them at a shop or you receive a phone call from them? This is an example of how our thoughts and feelings can bring things into reality.

I listened to The Vortex CD in my car on a regular basis and soaked up the teaching of Abraham. This has been engrained into my mind and is now becoming a default way of life for me.

Lesson: Letting Go and sending love energy

You cannot control others. We can only control ourselves. I realised that if you can't do anything about it, then you must let it go. Don't be a prisoner to the things you can't change.

Daily Affirmation
I feel tolerance and compassion and love for all people, myself included.

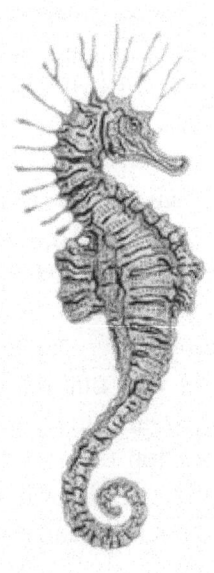

Chapter 6 : Self-Love

Inner child – Energy work

"Self respect. Self worth and self love all start with self. Stop looking outside of yourSELF for your value. "
~ Rob Liano

The most important project you will ever work on is YOU!

Throughout the last year I have worked on myself consistently and for what it seems a long time!

We never stop evolving, so the self-care and energy work should never stop.

Change is inevitable and is something we must embrace and not fight against.

To cope with change, we must do inner work on ourselves.

What I mean by energy work is soul work. We should release old past life and childhood and even recent years' experiences that have affected us. The only way to move on and stop repeating patterns is to let go of old stuff and make way for new stuff. It works similarly to de-cluttering your material possessions. If you leave space, then more can come in to your life. This works the same with experiences and relationships.

When we release old emotions and experiences, we can let go and move forward with new better experiences and relationships.

Ways to do this are to meditate, use guided ones if you want to, search for ones about letting go, or forgiveness of self and others. Or you can ask your angels and guides to come in and help you release and move on. There are many tools out there for doing this.

The simple way to do it is when any bad feelings come up that are of lower vibrations; such as anger, fear or sadness. We can ask why we are feeling this and think about what is making us feel this way. Then say to yourself that this no longer serves my highest good. With a grateful heart thank the universe for the experience and teachings. Then ask for it to be released and think about what you want in your life rather than what you didn't want.

Hypnosis
I also had a few hypnosis sessions with people that I know.
These helped me to realise which past experiences may still be holding me back in my life, and helped me to work on them.

Mirror Work
I also carried out some mirror work to help heal my inner child from past childhood pain. Limiting beliefs about yourself can be removed through doing this. It also helps you to love yourself more to improve your confidence and aids being comfortable being alone with yourself.

Look in the mirror and use the ho'oponopono words - calmly repeat 3 times... "I am sorry, please forgive me, I love you, thank you" thinking of self as you are now and of the little you as a child, also the person you wish to forgive or send love energy to. For example your mother or father or a past or existing partner. Stay quiet and wait to see if anything else arrives to be healed.

After saying this to myself in the mirror and looking deeply into my eyes (which are the windows to the soul) I sat down and used a guided meditation for forgiveness and letting go.

Within this meditation I felt a deep love in my heart and began to cry, this was me releasing past pain and feeling the love of forgiving others that had hurt me in the past.
A great exercise that left me feeling lighter and happier afterwards, as if I had been cleansed.

I also use pure quality essential oils to help my emotions and physical health. These really have amazing energy and work similarly to crystals and all other sources of nature that help us to feel grounded and at peace.

When it comes down to it, all there is in our reality is love and unity. If we focus on this and sending out love to ourselves and the world we really can make positive progress.

We can practise the self-love and sending love out when we are going through the many ups and downs of our existence.

For example, whenever my ex-husband seemed to be giving me a hard time and I could use these opportunities to see what he was reflecting to me.

My daughter's dad accused me of failing at relationships and that I had a short temper. This was telling me that one he was also guilty of these things and was trying to ease his guilt by sending this negative energy my way to make himself feel better.

More importantly, it showed me that I still had stuff to clear. Was I feeling like I had failed? Was I feeling that I was angry and short tempered? If so, then yes, I had to face them and do my best to release these low vibration feelings.

When I met his girlfriend for the first time and allowed my daughter to go away for the weekend with them, I used my new-found way of coping... sending love to them. This really worked and I actually enjoyed meeting her and felt very at ease when they drove away with my daughter for their trip away together.

I did not feel jealous that he had a relationship and I was on my own. I just felt love for them. I wished them the best.

If we stay in our heart space, nothing bad can get to us. It is as simple as that.

Dealing with being alone...
I had a very nice Sunday alone when my daughter was away with her daddy and is girlfriend.

After a lovely evening with a good friend the night before, I treated myself to a long lie in bed until 10am! Then went to my local health club for a relaxing swim and jacuzzi.

After getting refreshed I decided to go to a pub nearby and buy myself a big roast dinner and slowly enjoyed it. I sat next to several families and couples. Not once did I feel uncomfortable or resentful towards any of them.

I actually felt happy that I had the confidence and love for myself to do all these things by myself that many do with others and have never done alone. It felt very liberating and peaceful.

After this I took myself home and began writing more of this wonderful book that you are now reading.

Lesson: Love yourSELF

To achieve real happiness and peace is true life success. Loving your self is the most important life lesson for any of us to learn and to constantly practice every single day of your life.

Daily Affirmation
I love and appreciate and take care of myself. I am enough.

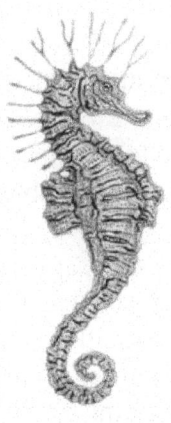

Chapter 7 : Help is at Hand

Feeling Let Down – Childhood blocks

"Energy flows where attention goes."
~ *Michael Beckwith*

I was fortunate enough to have an amazing client that was embarking on her new venture of becoming a Life Coach.

So, she offered me some free sessions to help her to complete her case studies for her training. Of course, I gracefully accepted and was pleased to be receiving this help just at the right time in my life.

This lovely lady was already a trained counsellor and had NLP training too. So, she was already very good at her chosen life path.

These sessions took place once a week for one hour at my house.

The first homework I was given was to write down 3 things a day that I felt I was doing well.

This really did help me to stay focused on a positive life path myself. To recognise the things, we are good at and acknowledge them by writing them down is an amazing tool that really lifts your spirit and brings more positive experiences your way.

The life coaching also helped me through both of my baby scans, where I had to face the father of the child now growing inside of me.

The life coach gave me some good tools to help me stay strong and feel good throughout these testing times.

Fortunately, all went smoothly with both scans and baby was developing very well. The father was kind and positive towards me too. I think the way I was behaving so nicely really helped the situation with the father.

Also, a friend of mine advised me to keep my heart open and to send love energetically towards the father, and this really did seem to make a big difference.

After these scans the father began communicating more and visited my home to help with jobs around the house that were becoming more difficult during pregnancy.

The only person that can truly make us feel good is ourselves.

When we feel let down by others it is usually mirroring back to us that we are in fact letting ourselves down.

I had many times when I felt let down by others, especially the male relationships in my life.

Through hypnosis, life coaching and much self-exploration and many times where I had been given this message by others when I had in fact seemed to be let down, I finally got the message that being let down had in fact come from my childhood, and I am sure many past life experiences too.

So, I spend an evening releasing this feeling and belief of being let down, and since have felt much better about this. So many of our relationships reflect ourselves. Both our dark and light sides can be seen in our network of friends.

We either choose to see it or we don't, however eventually we will be forced to face it whether we want to or not. So, we may as well choose to do the work and keep moving onwards and upwards so that our lives just go on improving.

Even our own children reflect things back to us. Being a parent is one of the most rewarding yet challenging journeys ever. It teaches you a lot about yourself.

Our children pick up on our energies and will reflect them back to us. So, if we are feeling relaxed and happy they too will be that way. Equally if we are feeling stressed or anxious they will be more difficult to look after, they become more agitated and will cause you to feel worse.

So, it is very important to realise how we can affect our child's behaviour. If we want an easier life, then we do need to look at ourselves and do the work to improve our ways so that our lives and our children's lives are easier and more enjoyable.

We must remember that we are worth it, we can be happy with just being ourselves.

Always focus more on the things we want from life, and take away our attention of the things we don't want.

One thing I have learnt that really has made a difference is to stay away from comparisons. Comparing our lives against the lives of others has never helped anyone.

Just because someone else appears to have everything that we want on the surface does not always mean that they are truly happy. We hope that they will be happy but we are never certain that they are. So, comparing our life with that of others is never healthy. It can only lead to disappointment and feelings of guilt and lack.

Lesson: Focus on your desire and be grateful

Focus on what you want and always be grateful and focused on what you already have. No matter how big or small that may be, your life is always great. Live in the present and you will always be happy and at peace.

Daily Affirmation

I create my own experiences. As I love and approve of myself and others, my experiences get better and better.

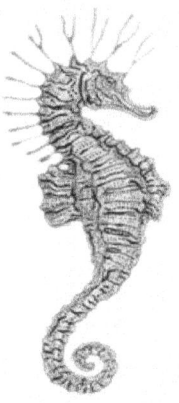

Chapter 8 : Roller Coasters

Divorce - Childcare

"What lies behind us, and what lies before us are small matters compared to what lies within us."
~ Ralph Waldo Emerson

There are many stages involved in leaving a marriage or relationship.

From sorting out finances to agreeing children's visits to meeting your ex's new partners.
There will always be challenges. Things we may be uncomfortable with facing.

However, if we step back from these each time they occur, and focus on the best outcome for the greatest good of all, then we really cannot go wrong.

Throughout all the pain from the past, I was always focused on the best results for my children.

However, we should also focus on obtaining the best for ourselves too.

Worrying and panicking in situations that feel so out of our control is never going to help us. The only way to deal with this is to step back and empower yourself by considering your options and finding the best alternative route forward for you and your family.

Often when a person attacks us, it is because they are either purging their own issues towards us or they are mirroring back to us our own past experiences that we have not dealt with.

For example, one time my ex-husband highlighted to me that my parents should be helping more with my daughter. He knew this was a sensitive subject for me, as I was always disappointed that my parents could not play a larger role in helping as grandparents. I often felt unsupported by them.

He was obviously trying to hurt me with this statement. However, he was also mirroring to me something that I still had not let go of. I needed to work through this to clear the energy related to this.

He also often communicated to me that he felt I was a failure because my new relationship after him had not worked out and I was left having the man's baby. He took great pleasure it seemed in saying these words to me.

It was probably just him mirroring me and the message was 'Do I think I am a failure?'

If so, then I needed to work on shifting this energy. When things like this come up that no longer serve our highest good it is always good to clear the energy connected to them.

Repeated patterns came along too, one in particular, was the weekly child maintenance that my husband had agreed to pay. He often paid it late and deducted money from it. I was constantly chasing him for the money and always left feeling let down. Also with regards to him visiting his daughter, he often showed up late and reduced the time I had to be child free and get some respite. This told me that I had issues around being 'let down' and issues around 'trust' and with attracting money into my life.

My life began to feel like a real struggle, battling to get money in to cover the bills and never having enough free time for doing things for myself.

I eventually had to take control back and ensure that I claimed all the benefits we were entitled to and did my very best to earn money through my small businesses. Trying hard not to rely on my exes. Covering all bases so I did not expect anything from them. If they gave any financial contributions or wanted to spend time with their children, I took this as a bonus!

Learning to keep the faith and to trust in the power of the universe to provide whenever the time came, was the best thing I could do.

Staying in a space of love and light and being grateful for all that I had (no matter how big or small) was the best way of coping.

I called in all resources, my support network of amazing spiritual friends and using all the energy tools I had learnt such as Meditation, oils, crystals, affirmations.

I also ensured that my children felt loved and secure, whatever was happening. It was so important to confirm that they were safe and I would always be there for them.

Working together as a team and including them completely in all of my life. I had to change my perception about freedom and me time. Realising that the only way for me not to feel trapped or controlled was to do my best for them. Being strict about food, behaviour and finances. Ensuring they respected all that we had. So, that nothing was wasted and everything was appreciated. These are the best lessons you could ever teach your children!

I also had to learn to be careful what I said in front of them, because there comes a time when they soak up all that we say and it is so important that we install the right information in their minds so they grow up balanced and happy.

We always have a CHOICE...

We either focus on being happy or being anything else but...

When we are experiencing adversity or pain in any form. What we must remember is to be present and instead of getting caught up in the emotions of the pain. We can choose to BREATHE. SMILE. LET GO. BE CALM.

We always have a CHOICE.

Be washed away in the pain and torment of what is happening to us.

Or let go of it, step back, be at peace.

Always choose peace.

Love is power

It is the higher vibration and is so much better to choose than to let our EGOS/MINDS sink us into NEGATIVITY.

When we are, ascending and evolving, we must try our very best to keep our frequency high.

The lower emotions just keep us in the third dimensional reality.

If we want more of the higher energy and emotions; happiness, love and joy then we must keep the continuity of remaining in those as often as we can.

Obviously, we all have off days and can feel sadness, and this is normal to shift the old patterns, and let go to enable our spiritual growth.

We are SOULS.

SOULS come from the HEART always.

EGO comes from the MIND. So, get out of your HEAD and step back into your HEART.

Meditate. Do things that make your heart sing. Be with people that raise your vibrations.

Surround yourself with joyful experiences.

YOU CAN DO IT.

EMPOWER YOURSELF.

LET GO and MOVE FORWARD.

Say GOODBYE to negativity and say HELLO to positivity.

Lesson: Do The Things that keep your energy high

Meditate. Breathe. Use tools such as crystals, oils, shells, nature and exercise as well as getting involved with activities that make your heart sing. Be with people that raise your vibrations. Surround yourself with joyful experiences. Meet with your creative self at least once a week. When your energy is high you can achieve so much more!

Daily Affirmation
I am enthusiastic about life and filled with energy and enthusiasm.

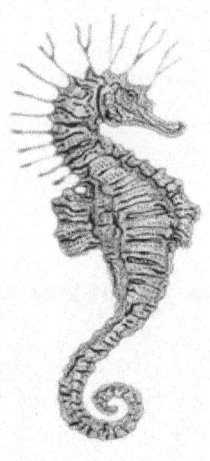

Chapter 9 : The Seahorse

Being both parents – Support groups

*"The monotony and solitude of a quiet life stimulates
the creative mind."*
~ *Albert Einstein*

The most difficult part about being a solo parent is that
being both parents, both Mum and Dad, is not that
simple. In fact, it is almost impossible.

We all know that a child does need both parents, a
Mum and a Dad. They need role models to look up to.
To learn from and to be balanced in the female and
male energy.

I found the challenges came when my child was
being particularly awkward in their behaviour. For
example, when you want your child to do something,
like going to bed on time and getting ready for school.
Or eating their dinner.

Your child knows it is only you and they test the
boundaries more because there is not another parent
there to enforce more power when it comes to the battle
of getting children to do the things you want them to
do.

It helps to have the support there from another
parent to back you up when your child is acting up.

Someone to say 'please listen to your mother/ father' or 'Do not say that to your mother/father'.

Instead you have to do this yourself. It is not always easy. However, it is possible and I succeeded many times by just talking calmly with my child and explaining why you need them to do a certain thing or why they shouldn't act a certain way.

Children are just little adults, they need nurturing, they need listening to, understanding and love goes a long way. An unlimited supply of patience also helps!

I found that my friends helped me many times when it came to making parenting easier. They gave me guidance and support that was invaluable along the way.

I learnt early on that building my friends network and keeping that strong was very important. Asking for help also did not come easy to begin with, but as time went by I soon became more comfortable with this and realised that it was the way to keep my sanity!

Single parenting is a real journey of self-discovery, learning so many lessons that you may not have learnt whilst in the co-dependent relations of the conventional marriage. The old paradigm of relationships are filled with obligations and not really based on unconditional where people do things because they want to and are not expected to do things.

Our new paradigm for relationships where we let go and set our partners free to discover their deep selves, finding their purpose and if they are meant for us they will come back, but not because they are obligated to do so, but because they are meant to be with you, out of choice, out of real deep soulful love.

So many times, in our lives, we miscommunicate with others because we put conditions on the relationships we share. Also, our minds can often rule our hearts. Our issues arise and need to be dealt with and not just brushed under the carpet to resurface again and again until they are dealt with.

When we spend time alone we work on ourselves (well hopefully we do!) Time apart is often a real healer and can bring people together into a greater partnership than they would have had before.

In September, I went to visit a Reiki Sea Energy Healer in the Farnborough area. I had met this woman two years ago at a holistic event that I took part in myself to promote my essential oils.

This lady has been healing for over twenty years. She takes her inspiration from the ocean and all sea life. Using sea shells and energy she can shift energy to help you release past emotions that often keep us stuck and do not enable us to move forward freely.

I discovered through the sea healer, that I too was attracted to this kind of healing. All my life I have carried a deep love and fascination for all things sea and beach. I have also always been attracted to the sea creature, the seahorse. This particular animal represents stability and the ability to hold on when times get rough. It attaches its tail to a rock or shell when the waters get stormy.

I also found out my life mission/ lesson is TRUST. Which was very interesting as most of my experiences in life so far have taught me a lot about this subject.

With only 6 or 7 weeks to go until I give birth to this baby boy growing in my womb, I write this with real passion, to get my story out there, and to help others that go through similar challenges in life. If my experience can help others, then there was a real purpose for my struggles.

Throughout my journey as a solo parent, I met many new friends, who are also solo parents that have had their fair share of struggles and have risen to the challenges as they arose.

A common trait ran throughout all these people, and that was strength, these people doing parenting alone are courageous and brave. They are loving but strong. They set their boundaries and stick to them. We must be prepared to say no to things and to say yes to things along the way. You must always stand up for what you believe in and you certainly should set standards to protect yourself and your children.

If you set your boundaries and stay true to them life is so much easier.

What I also found is that what seems bad is often not true, and reality is often what we perceive from our insecurities.

Once we learn to love, be open and let go of attachments of all kinds we truly start living a simpler life.

So many of us try so hard to control everything in our lives and often the outcome is not what we wanted. So, when we start letting go and just going with the flow our lives seem to get so much easier.

The solo journey is often portrayed as lonely, but it is also very comforting because it gives us a chance to reflect on our lives and learn that all the answers are within, and those times of solitude can give us the most clarity and greatest life lessons if we allow ourselves quiet time to go within and truly connect with our higher selves.

Loving ourselves is the most important lesson and it is the only way we will ever achieve all we want in our lives.

I truly have made the best friends on my solo journey in this one year I have been separated from my ex-husband.

It seems that when we go through adversity we gain respect from so many people, and showing our vulnerability we connect with so many and that is when we make the best relations we will ever make, because people see our true beings and we see theirs. Connection is made at a deep level and that is precious.

The battles I faced with my ex-husband over contact with my daughter, financial support and responsible parenting, were tough. Often I was left feeling sad and guilt ridden when she left with her dad. I didn't trust him. Always felt insecure and worried that she wouldn't be safe.

Eventually I had to learn to detach and let go, and just trust that she would be safe, that she could protect herself, that the universe would ensure she was protected. I truly had to practice faith and believe that she would always be returned to me safely and that she would be happy.

Time is a healer, and this is very true. Eventually things do get better, but it takes learning and patience and a great deal of faith.

When it comes down to it, all we can do is control ourselves, our own lives, the way we feel and anything outside of ourselves is never in our control, all we can do is send positive vibes and believe in positive outcomes.

Lesson: Solitude is time to go within and realise our true potential

The solo journey is often portrayed as lonely, but it is also very comforting because it gives us a chance to reflect on our lives and learn that all the answers are within. Times of solitude can give us the most clarity and greatest life lessons if we allow ourselves quiet time to go within and truly connect with our higher selves.

Daily Affirmation
It is safe for me to see. I am at peace.

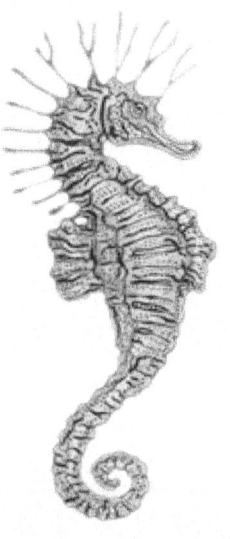

Chapter 10 : Feeling Good

The strength within – Growth and gratitude

"Something inside you emerges… an innate indwelling peace, stillness, aliveness. It is the unconditioned, who you are in your essence. It is what you had been looking for in the love object. It is yourSELF. "
~ Eckhart Tolle

Throughout this journey of the last eight months; I have learnt more in this year than I have in my whole life.

2016 has been a year of endings and new beginnings. In my darkest times, I have made the most growth and change.

I have moved house this year, spent most of the year pregnant, going through divorce and have a new relationship with myself and the father of my baby.

This is a lot of change and experiences for one person in less than one year.

Many times, I have felt close to breakdown and the tears have flowed so much that I could have filled a full-size swimming pool by now.

However, I have made the best friends and grown the strongest support network I could have ever wished for.

I have learnt so much about myself, and accepted the dark and light within me. This took a lot of work using energy techniques and keeping track of the full moons and new moons and super moons so I could do letting go and manifestations to release the old and bring in the new for the greater good of all.

While I write this, it is now October 18th and I am 37 weeks pregnant.

I have been a solo mother for the last 7 months and have developed one hell of a bond with my five-year-old daughter. Fought many battles with my ex-husband and have been juggling the finances within an inch of their life!

It has been a rollercoaster of emotions and growth.

On 16th October, the father of my baby came to see me. After many meet ups through scans and midwife appointments where it seemed we were just friends and keeping communications open for the baby. We finally met up on Sunday 16 October on the weekend of the super moon in Aries. This just so happens to be his star sign. Which is quite amazing.

The same day my daughter went off with her daddy to her nanny's birthday get together and this was a turning point to me standing up to him and deciding best route for my daughter and all involved is that she does not see him any longer.

After she left I was in floods of tears and felt hysterical. This was a dark moment. The ones they tell you will be turning points that make you stronger. This was one of those moments.

Soon after this happened my light of my life the father of my baby showed up and took me out for dinner. He held my hand across the table and sincerely apologised for disappearing for 7 months and asked if there would be any way I would accept him back into our lives. He has missed me and wants to make a go of things with me, the baby and my daughter.

It was a very special moment. I felt excited, nervous and cautious but also very positive about this. I realised for months now that he and I may well be twin flames and have a very special purpose on this planet. To bring much love and light to the world to help heal the collective.

We have a very 'go with the flow and non-conventional relationship', where we give each other the right amount of space to do our own things. This is essential for our journey together so we can both grow and evolve for our mission.

I told him that I think we needed that 7 month break apart to both release our issues and grow. We have now come back together stronger and more ready for our path together. We have reunited to serve our mission as twin flames and to bring up our little family of two children that are very special twin flame souls too. They need us as parents for their missions too.

It has all become very clear now and all the past hurts are worthwhile because without sacrifice nothing is gained. Pain is a required part of life to help us grow.

Those 7 months have served us well and we are now in a position to really work as a team and support one another to be unstoppable on our very important life purpose.

Love really is the greatest power on this earth, and it can rise above any dark force. The energy that real pure soul love that is unconditional can glow strong and cannot be distinguished.

Our flame is bright and will burn for eternity. LOVE IS TRUE AND PURE... AND SO, IT IS

Lesson: Unconditional Love – fully accepting self – Take back your power

Love is the most powerful energy on the planet, it can heal anything. Real love is unconditional which means loving without expectations or obligations to be or do anything. Loving without expecting another to give that love back or to do anything for you. That is real Love. It is co-creative love it is not codependent love. Depending on others for anything is not real. It is an illusion. We must love ourselves unconditionally. Fully accepting our dark and light sides. If you can fully love everything about yourself. Then Love has Won! If we can love and let go and give as much freedom to another as we give ourselves then we have real unconditional love – the purest form of love there is!

Daily Affirmation
I lovingly take back my power and eliminate all interference.

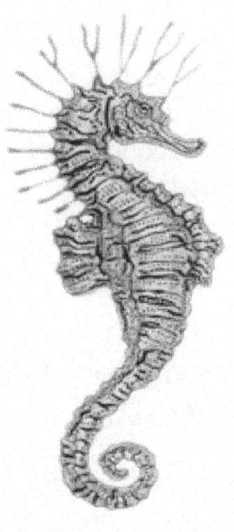

Chapter 11 : Birth Stories

Zara: famous 5 minutes – Xander: little rocket

"You feel your strength in the experience of pain."
~ Jim Morrison

Birth of my first child – my daughter (I wrote the I Am Well book whilst pregnant with Zara)

Zara Philippa Walker Born 02.06.11 12.08 midday weighing 6lbs 7oz

On midnight of the 1st June I was sick...

At 3am, contractions start (mild period pains)

Husband wakes to my moaning and says 'has it started yet? - great this will be our proudest moment!' 5am get out of bed and call my hypnobirthing partner Juliet

At 7am, Juliet arrives with pineapple, straws and energy tablets and an iPad computer to time contractions on! Contractions are 3-4 minutes apart!

At 7.30am, call midwife who comes at 8am and does a check and finds I am 3cm dilated already!

At 8.30am, contractions get stronger, deep lower back pain and feeling of pressure in bottom (Lots of positions using gym ball and husband for support)

At 10am, waters break husband fills the birthing pool!

At 10.15am, sit on toilet trying to urinate!

At 10.30am, get in pool (what a relief to the pressure of contractions! - wow!) Two Midwives arrive I zone out into my meditation mode using my breathing and hypnosis visualisations to ease pressure and keep relaxed

At 11am, pushing contractions begin and things hot up (Husband gets cold wet flannel for my face and mops my brow!) Head is crowning, a few strong contractions and pushes and babies head is out by around

At 11.45am, contractions slowed down so midwife used clary sage oil on a flannel wiping around chest and head also allowing me to inhale the essence! Within minutes the strong pushing contractions came that helped me to deliver baby Zara into the water (Clary sage oil really does work!)

They placed her on my chest at 12.08pm midday and her Dad cut the cord (and cried lots!) - I said 'hello baby Zara' and could not believe that I had done it – what a feeling of relief and joy!

I delivered the placenta in the pool and immediately after this was put into a Tupperware box and placed in fridge until my placenta encapsulation lady came to collect later for making into capsules for me to take each day (huge benefits for health of baby and mother!)

A relaxed natural (only pain relief was breathing and water) home pool and hypnobirthing (highly recommended - I would do it again!) No stitches to perineal either! Just a little 1st degree tear that will heal on its own.

Zara Philippa Walker is the light of our lives and truly the greatest gift we could ever wish for. We are eternally grateful.

This was a wonderful experience and not at all like the horror stories most women tell of childbirth!

Second child - my son (wrote this book whilst pregnant with Xander)
Xander Henry Cooke Born 12.11.16 3.58pm weighing 8lbs

At 11.11am on Saturday 12th November 2016, my contractions began as very mild wave like surges throughout my body. Very mild period like pains.

These went on for a little while, and I laid down with the love of my life. We hugged and enjoyed our alone time at the start of our journey of welcoming our baby boy into our lives. A nice steady start. I even made pizzas whilst having these waves.

Around 1pm, the contractions began to become stronger. I walked around the house and leant on my bed whilst swaying my hips.

At around 3pm, I messaged my doula Zara to let her know that I was feeling a little scared as contractions were strong and I could feel my lower parts becoming open.

At 3.20pm, Zara made her way to me.

I climbed on bed after my waters had broken on my bedroom carpet.

I held myself up in an all fours position. This felt the natural way to be. Very raw and primal.

I started to shake all over partly with fear but also adrenaline rushing through me.
I could feel every movement of my baby coming through me. He was in a rush to journey into this world. It was a feeling of I am on this rollercoaster and there is no getting off this ride now. I was facing many fears, such as giving birth on dry land without the aid of the water for pain relief. No medical people around me as midwife was clearly not going to make it in time.

My loving partner and my beautiful daughter Zara were by my side. In fact, the father was right behind me getting a full view of his son being born into this world.

Next I felt someone pounce onto the bed next to me! It was my doula. She was like wonder-woman; in fact, we now call her "Superdoula"!

She put her arms around me and said you can do it Cheryl! I screamed FUCK and felt my baby boy crowning, and the next time he was pushing his head right through and I felt the ring of fire, burn, burn, burn his way out of me. Oh my, I had not felt this extreme pain when I'd had Zara because I was relaxed more with the water.

This dry land birth was raw and totally natural. The best birth yet. However, it was the most terrifying one. The trauma you feel with a quick birth is quite overwhelming. Very powerful and extremely tiring. However still very positive.

The father caught his beautiful baby boy in his hands. He said it was truly amazing to see and experience this wonderful and powerful arrival of his first-born son. My love was a very proud daddy indeed! He was so calm; I am very proud of the father. This has cemented our love, the experience of seeing each other in our true power was quite breath-taking.

So, lovely for my daughter to experience the birth of her baby brother too. She is a very proud big sister.

It took twenty minutes' active labour to birth our son Xander. However, it took longer to birth the placenta afterwards, which was good as the whole time we kept him attached to his cord so he could experience the delayed cord clamping benefits to his health.

Unfortunately, I did experience some tearing on my perineum due to the quickness of his arrival. So, had to be stitched up by the midwife, which hurt slightly, however this was part of the process of clearing my fears around this too.

Xander was certainly bringing out a lot of my fears to be cleared. So, this is good as I now feel even more empowered as goddess woman in this physical dimension.

Lesson: Childbirth is a natural positive experience

Both my children were born naturally without any pain relief. I proved to myself that childbirth can be a positive experience and not the hell that society leads us to believe. It's a case of mind over matter. My mother told me of her nightmare experiences and many tell of their hellish birth stories. We do not have to go with conditioning. We can find our own way. Just re-program your mind and you can do anything the way you wish for it to happen.

Daily Affirmation
I relax knowing I am safe. Life trusts me, and I trust the process of life.

Chapter 12 : Self-Love

Runner and Chaser – Dynamic twin flames

"The broken will always be able to love harder than most.
Once you've been in the dark you learn to appreciate everything that shines."
~ Zachary K Douglas

Our evolved relationship was going really well. We could not keep our hands off each other and that was leading up to our child's birth and even three weeks after he was born! There is clearly much passion in our twin flame union. Sometimes this can be overwhelming for both involved. The flames burn so bright that at times it can be quite intense.

We enjoyed a loving happy Christmas and New Year together as a family and even though we had a new-born child taking our energy, we still found much time and energy for each other.

The first 6 to 12 weeks of Xander's life were truly challenging! He has major colic and many energetic issues which he had held from the stresses of my pregnancy and the very swift birth into this world!

We took him to see a cranial osteopath who also works with energy. She was able to correct his physical issues but also help calm his energy.
Xander cried constantly and really showed us he was here!

On 12th January, my love and I celebrated our first anniversary of when we first met!

On this day though I felt it adequate to talk of our life together and how we could achieve balance and plan our future. He seemed happy about the truth that was spoken. However later that day Xander was playing up and we got stressed with each other, and shouted at one another for the first time ever!

That night we made love and it was the deepest and closest we had become since our reunion. It was as if we had merged as one.

Later that night, Xander fed and cried often. I became stressed and tired. My love shouted at me 'Just Be a Mother' and went down to the sofa to sleep!

The next day...

The strain of the crying and late nights took its toll on our relationship.

On 13th January, my love decided not to come back to us. He sent a few texts saying he was feeling moody and did not want to fight in front of the children.

I was hysterical and felt like he had died, my intuition told me that he had run again, and this time it cut deeper than before. I felt as if a sharp blade had been driven through my whole body. I cried in child pose on the bathroom floor. The energy had to shift. Lucky for me my friend Nikki was here and she looked after my children while I had a mini breakdown upstairs!

I heard nothing from him for weeks. Then heard from social services. Saying they had a report that I was not looking after my baby correctly!

I was shocked to find out that my love may have reported me to Child Services, and felt very disappointed. However, I can see why he did it, it was out of fear, he saw I was not coping and he certainly wasn't coping. He called them because he didn't know what else to do.

Since then he has paid maintenance for Xander each week into my bank account. However, we have had no contact.

My heart felt ripped out and torn ever since he left. The best way to ease this pain is to love yourself and live with grateful heart and be kind to yourself and others.

Every day I am learning to 'Be a Mother' and to love myself and truly accept myself and my life as it is now.

Lessons:
To be a Mother – Just Love them
Love myself – be happy within
Gratitude – for all I have now
Slow down – baby steps
Stay present – be in the now
Stop projecting
Stay in my heart
Focus on me
Only think about what I want

Stop running from myself
Face my shadow side
Accept all of me
Laugh and accept all the perceived badness
Stop doubting myself
Believe I am good enough
I can have what I want
Everything is okay as it is now
Just BE

Daily Affirmation...
I love and accept myself just as I am

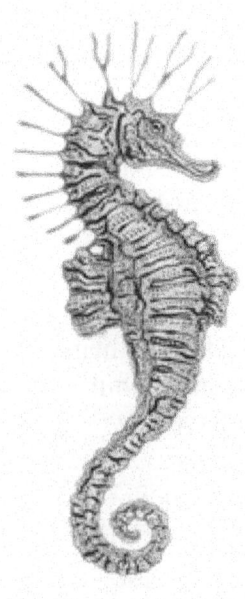

Chapter 13 : My Life Path

Helping mothers and children –

Health, inspiration and wellness

"The greatest wealth is health"
~ Virgil

For many years, I have known that I was different, and always felt I was on the outside looking in.

At school, I was not a popular child, and in fact I was bullied badly by a group of girls.
I always felt alone and stood out from the crowd. Years later I discovered that I had healing hands when I decided to train as a massage therapist.

My journey now as a healer and empath, is still not an easy one, however it can be very rewarding and although it is often unforgiving, it is my destiny and I must stay true to this life path.

I have always been compelled to help others, with a caring attitude towards all life forms including the trees and plants. I have never been able to hurt any life form. I always felt deep sadness and sick if I observed any form of cruelty to an animal or person.

My mother was always negative and it seemed she was often unwell when I was growing up. I think this is maybe why I discovered the natural health path. I didn't want my life to be like hers. I became interested in wellness before my daughter was born in June 2011.

I began filtering my water and taking supplements in about 2008. My health was so greatly improved before I became pregnant with my first child. Which meant that my pregnancies and my children were all healthy.

I feel very proud of my health and spiritual journey so far, and I am committed to continued lifelong learning around these subjects.

From using plant medicine (oils) to meditation and body mind and soul self-talk to heal the cells of the body. You name it, I believe that we can self-heal it.

Cleaning up our diets to eradicate sugar, wheat and dairy also helps greatly. To be honest a raw vegan diet is the ideal for our digestive systems.

I have written this book to help inspire other parents that find themselves parenting alone. It is a difficult but rewarding journey and I do believe that part of the reason we find ourselves in this situation is to make us stronger, to break through the old paradigm and conventional conditioning that we have been shown over the years. We are here to re-learn and practice the new paradigm way. Living unconditionally without demands and obligations. Living from our hearts, with pure love and true intentions.

Lesson: Realising your soul purpose

Our conditioning through life leads us to our true life path. Mine was to teach about natural health due to my mother's negative view of life and wellness, believing she was always unwell. Our experiences help us grow and realise our soul purpose.

Daily Affirmation
I am one with ALL OF LIFE. I am safe at all times.

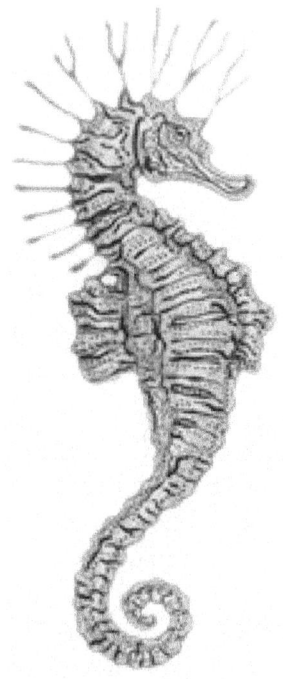

Chapter 14 : Friends Indeed

Support network – Love and gratitude

*"Health is the greatest gift, contentment the greatest
wealth, faithfulness the best
relationship."*
~ Buddha

I have discovered during this journey as a solo mother
bringing up my two extraordinary children that my
friends, the ones that are true have been there and
helped me to stay strong and to realise so many lessons
that have made me stronger and enabled me to love
myself and my children greater than I could have ever
wished for.

However even though friends are a godsend and I
am truly grateful for all of my dear soulmates. I have
come to realise they are a mirror of our own self, our
soul. They are facets of our personality and that it is
ourselves / our soul that truly helps us.

Coming to know that we are actually only here with
ourselves was a real deep realisation and it lifted me to
know that we are not alone, because we have ourselves
and that is all the real company we need.

It is empowering to know that we are the creator of
our reality and we can truly have anything we want; we
just have to realise it. When we realise that everything
that happens to us is in fact created by us at whatever

level, be it conscious or unconscious. It begins to make sense. Then it doesn't feel so bad.

It is comforting to know that we are never truly alone. We always have ourselves. We are our own best friend, our lover, our mother, our teacher, our only requirement for a happy life.

When you just accept yourself fully for all that you are, and realise that just being your true self really is enough, things really start to change.

Over thinking was always my biggest downfall in my life.

Meditating, walks in nature, swimming, socialising, loving my children, loving myself, being grateful, writing and being creative have all enhanced my life.

I can now be who I am meant to be. I can now be ME. I can now enjoy and appreciate my life. I am now truly free and happy where I am NOW.

Thank you to all my teachers, all the my relationships, all my mirrors - to you I am truly GRATEFUL. If we truly love ourselves and others, we set them and ourselves free. If it is meant to be for our life journey, then it will always come back to us.

Lesson: We create every experience

Every experience and relationship in our lives is our creation. They act as a mirror to teach us what we are here to learn. We learn and we move on. What is meant to stay in our lives, will stay. What is meant to go will go. It is that simple.

From your HEART - Enjoy the journey – Love yourSELF – Be Grateful

Daily Affirmation

I lovingly take care of my body, my mind, and my emotions.

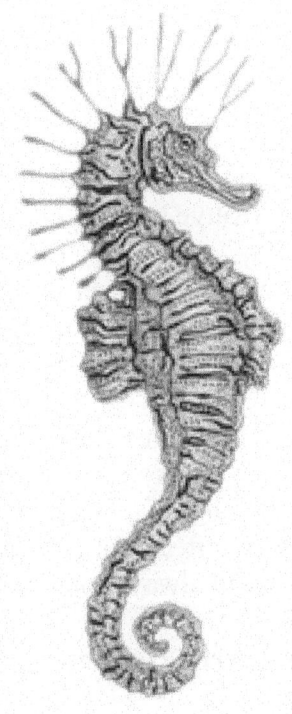

Acknowledgements

Being grateful and giving thanks for all in your life is the most cleansing and self-caring practice we can do so here we go...

I am truly thankful to all my friends and professionals that have helped me throughout my life journey so far…

My dear friends…

Shirley Cole my longest and dearest friend, who I met years ago when I was in my deep depression period. She gave me some amazing life coaching sessions and years later we are still friends and she is still coaching me! She gives great advice about how energy works and is always very truthful and honest with me. Thank you, lovely lady.

Doug New for his advice and words on magic and energy and his valuable time in caring for my children when my batteries required a recharge. I got some important ME Time out enjoying my favourite leisure; swimming and indulged my love of the water.

Jen Thomas: The Confidence Coach for her amazing life coaching skills and good company on some walks in nature.

Deborah and Richard Knight, thank you for your continued support and for being such an amazing family to admire and aspire to as co-creative dynamic couple.

Nikki Marianna Hope for her shamanic healing KKI essences and drumming workshops. We connected the moment we met at a spiritual fair and she has helped my family greatly.

Jeanne Witt, I just love your amazing sea healing at faery whispers; She opened my eyes to a whole new world of sea energy and the mermaid seahorse journey I'm now on.

Amazingly too I'd like to thank the fathers of my two children as they pushed my buttons and enabled me to do the healing that my soul needed for my life journey. They also helped blessed me with two amazing children in my life. Which leads me on to thanking my two children Zara and Xander for teaching me about being a parent and highlighting my issues that come up to be healed. I love you my beautiful children and I love all my friends and connections on my life journey.

Thank you I am eternally grateful to all of you.

If you are reading this and I have not mentioned your name, please don't think you're not valued as much as you are all connected to me as we are all one and just mirrors of one another and I feel you in my heart and soul. Thank you.

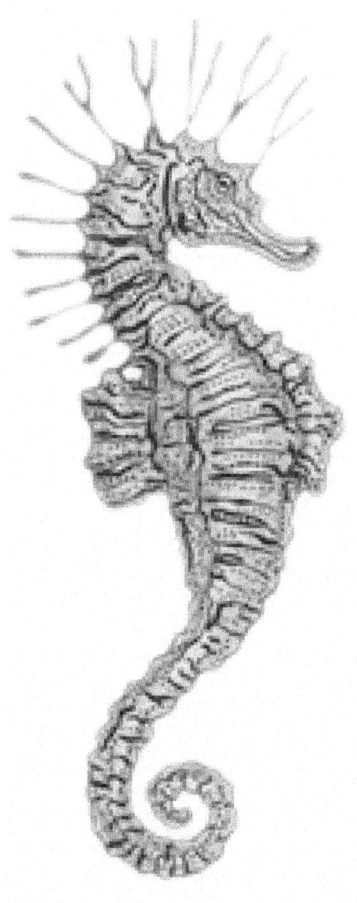

About the Author : Cheryl Cooke

Cheryl was born in 1975 into a farming background. Her family are good honest hard working country folk. In 2011, Cheryl became a mother to her first child; her beautiful daughter Zara.

Becoming a solo parent in 2015. She wrote her second book whilst pregnant with her second child; her son Xander who was born in November 2016. In both pregnancies, she birthed a new book each time. Her first one 'I Am Well – A World Free of Dis-ease' talking about all wellness and life issues.

Cheryl runs a health and wellness business as healer and therapist and teaches parents about natural plant medicine to keep the whole family healthy.

Cheryl has aspirations of inspiring the next generation to live naturally and spiritually. Her mission is to teach parents that their children can live healthy lives by boosting their immune systems and balancing their energies.

She is a peacekeeper by heart and wants to give the best to the world whilst enjoying her family life. She still believes that love is the most powerful energy on this earth and hopes that one day she lives with her life partner in her off the grid beach home to fulfil her love for nature and the sea. Her mission is to inspire other parents that you can find your inner strength to be empowered to live the best life possible.

Ferapi – Therapy and Massage
http://www.ferapi.com

doTerra Oils (plant medicine)
http://www.mydoterra.com/cherylcooke1

For daily updates, video blogs and continued health advice to help your parenting, wellness and spiritual journey, visit :

The Empowered Solo Parent Group Page
https://www.facebook.com/empoweredsoloparent/

Clean Living – I Am Well Group Page
https://www.facebook.com/groups/cleanlivingiamwell/

After Words

Strangely Incomprehensible : About the Seahorse

Just when we think we understand the world and how it works, something can come along to turn our ideas of how things work on their head. The seahorse demonstrates this admirably, being odd in two respects.

Firstly as it swims upright while virtually all other fish swim horizontally. Only the razorfish swims in a similar fashion.

The second strange thing about seahorses is how they reproduce. They court for several days. During this time, they change colour, swim side by side holding tails and gripping the same strand of sea grass. They often wheel around in unison in a dance which can last up to eight hours.

During this dance the male pumps water through the egg pouch on his trunk which expands and opens to display its emptiness. The female inserts her ovipositor into the male's brood pouch and deposits thousands of eggs. As the female releases her eggs, her body slims while his swells. Both animals then sink back into the seagrass and she swims away.

Nobody quite knows what the female seahorse does after leaving the male to hold the babies. She is obviously a mistress of her elements.

The latin name for seahorse is hippocampus which comes from hippo meaning horse and campus meaning sea monster. Some of them are over fourteen inches in height and very dragon-like.

Inside our heads are two seahorse-shaped structures, one on each side of the brain, also called the hippocampus.

It is perhaps strangely coincidental that the role of the hippocampus seems to be to help us make sense of the world. It even lights up when it detects something out of the ordinary. It encodes and makes sense of memories and creates a navigational map of the world. This is not necessarily a physical atlas. It is a map of how the world works and how we fit into it. Dementia sets in when this part of the brain degenerates.

Just by reading these words, the two oddities about aquatic hippocampi have holographically been mirrored inside your own hippocampi.

Now that is strangely incomprehensible.

Republished from The Germinatrix and Other Tall Tales with kind permission of Tom Evans

Review from a reader on Amazon:

I really enjoyed this book. Read the whole book in one afternoon on my Kindle. I think Cheryl's honesty and her account of her experiences of being a solo parent would be helpful and supportive to anyone in a similar situation. Highly recommend this book.

9 781787 231351